IMAGES OF WAR
THE GERMAN ARMY ON CAMPAIGN 1914-1918

RARE PHOTOGRAPHS FROM WARTIME ARCHIVES

IMAGES OF WAR
THE GERMAN ARMY ON CAMPAIGN 1914-1918

RARE PHOTOGRAPHS FROM WARTIME ARCHIVES

BOB CARRUTHERS

Pen & Sword
MILITARY

This edition published in 2016 by

Pen & Sword Military
An imprint of
Pen & Sword Books Ltd.
47 Church Street
Barnsley
South Yorkshire
S70 2AS

ISBN: 9781473837829

A CIP catalogue record for this book is available from the British Library.

Printed and bound in England
By CPI Group (UK) Ltd., Croydon, CR0 4YY

Pen & Sword Books Ltd. incorporates the imprints of Pen & Sword Aviation, Pen & Sword Family History, Pen & Sword Maritime, Pen & Sword Military, Pen & Sword Discovery, Pen & Sword Politics, Pen & Sword Atlas, Pen & Sword Archaeology, Wharncliffe Local History, Wharncliffe True Crime, Wharncliffe Transport, Pen & Sword Select, Pen & Sword Military Classics, Leo Cooper, The Praetorian Press, Claymore Press, Remember When, Seaforth Publishing and Frontline Publishing

For a complete list of Pen & Sword titles please contact

PEN & SWORD BOOKS LIMITED
47 Church Street, Barnsley, South Yorkshire, S70 2AS, England
E-mail: enquiries@pen-and-sword.co.uk
Website: www.pen-and-sword.co.uk

The German Army On Campaign 1914-1918

The men who look back at us from the pages of this book were members of the German Army. Unlike the British and French armies against whom these men were pitched during the Great War, it is an institution which no longer exists. The German Army enjoyed a relatively brief incarnation, it was formed after the unification of Germany under Prussian leadership in 1871, and was dissolved in 1919, following the defeat of the German Empire in the Great War. The men pictured within these pages knew the force in which they served as the *Deutsches Heer* or German Army, which was the name given to the combined land and air forces of Germany.

It is important to understand that the German Army was not a heterogeneous institution. It was comprised of four major elements drawn from the major states of Germany, each of which had its own distinct character and traditions. Shortly after the outbreak of the Franco-Prussian War in 1870, the North German Confederation had entered into a series of conventions on military matters in order to regularise military matters with states that were not members of the confederation. The largest of the semi-autonomous states within the German Empire namely Bavaria, Württemberg, Saxony and Baden were to provide the four major non-Prussian elements of the German Army with Bavaria providing the largest contingent. In times of peace the contingents of the Bavarian, Saxon and Württemberg kingdoms were independent entities, however in times of war the Prussian Army assumed almost total control over the armies of the other states of the Empire.

Despite taking their marching orders from Berlin, the Bavarian, Saxon and Württemberg armies maintained distinct identities. Each kingdom had its own War Ministry. Bavaria and Saxony published their own rank and seniority lists for their officers and Württemberg's list was a separate chapter of the Prussian army rank lists. Württemberg and Saxon units were numbered according to the Prussian system, but Bavarian units maintained their own numbering system (thus, the 2nd Württemberg Infantry Regiment was Infantry Regiment No. 120 under the Prussian system).

The largest of the four armies was the Bavarian Army. It had formed the army of the Electorate of Bavaria from 1682-1806 and then the Kingdom of Bavaria from 1806 onwards. It therefore existed from 1682 as the standing army of Bavaria until the merger of the military sovereignty of Bavaria into that of the German State in 1919. However, the Bavarian army was never comparable in size to the armies of the Great Powers of the 19th century, but it did provide the Bavarian Wittelsbach dynasty with sufficient scope of action to transform Bavaria from a territorially-disjointed small state to the second-largest state of the German Empire after Prussia. The Bavarian Army was a marginally less egalitarian outfit than the hidebound Prussian army. Since the dissolution in 1826 of the Lifeguard unit, there was no specific Guard regiment and as a result the Bavarian Army boasted a noticeably smaller proportion of aristocratic officers than the Prussian Army. In 1914 there were six officers drawn from common stock for every nobleman who held a commission.

The overall commander of the German Army in peacetime, less the Bavarian contingent, was the Kaiser. He was assisted by a German Imperial Military Cabinet, and exercised control through the Ministry of War and the Great General Staff. The Chief of the General Staff became the Kaiser's main military advisor and effectively the most powerful military figure in the Empire. Bavaria maintained its own Ministry of War and its own Royal Bavarian Army General Staff, but coordinated planning with the Prussian Great General Staff.

The command and control system of the Prussian Army had been heavily reformed in the wake of the defeats suffered by Prussia in the Napoleonic Wars. The General Staff system, an institution that sought to institutionalize military excellence, was the main result. It sought to identify military talent at the lower levels and develop it thoroughly through academic training and practical experience as principal staff officers on division, corps and higher staffs, up to the Great General Staff, the senior planning body of the army. It provided effective planning and organisational work during peacetime and wartime. The Prussian General Staff, proven in battle in the Wars of Unification, became effectively the German General Staff upon formation of the German Empire, given Prussia's leading role in the German Army.

The basic peacetime organisational structure of the German Army was based around the Army inspectorate (*Armee-Inspektion*), the army corps (*Armeekorps*), the division, and the regiment. During wartime, the staff of the Army inspectorates formed field army commands, which controlled the corps and subordinate units. During the Great War, a higher command level, the army group (*Heeresgruppe*), was created. Each army group controlled several field armies.

At the outbreak of the Great War Germany was divided into eight army inspectorates, each of which oversaw three or four corps.

I Army Inspectorate: Headquartered in Danzig, became the Eighth Army on mobilisation (2 August 1914)

II Army Inspectorate: Headquartered in Berlin, became the Third Army on mobilisation (2 August 1914)

III Army Inspectorate: Headquartered in Hannover, became the Second Army on mobilisation (2 August 1914)

IV Army Inspectorate: Headquartered in Munich, became the Sixth Army on mobilisation (2 August 1914)

V Army Inspectorate: Headquartered in Karlsruhe, became the Seventh Army on mobilisation (2 August 1914)

VI Army Inspectorate: Headquartered in Stuttgart, became the Fourth Army on mobilisation (2 August 1914)

VII Army Inspectorate: Headquartered in Berlin, became the Fifth Army on mobilisation (2 August 1914)

VIII Army Inspectorate: Headquartered in Saarbrücken, became the First Army on mobilisation (2 August 1914)

Although it was outnumbered and surrounded by enemies on all sides the Imperial German Army fought doggedly from August 1914 until the armistice of 1918. In the course of the fighting it managed to defeat the Imperial Russian Army in 1917 and, technically at least, it could be argued that it was never defeated in the field. This tenuous assumption was to form the basis of the *Dolchstoßlegende*, which was the notion, widely believed in army circles in Germany after 1918, that the German Army was betrayed by the civilians on the home front. One of the chief advocates of this theory was a lance corporal from the ranks of the Bavarian Army by the name of Adolf Hitler.

The capitulation of 1918 was blamed by Hitler and others upon the unpatriotic populace, the Socialists, Bolsheviks and especially the Jews. By the time the Nazis came to power in 1933 they made the legend an integral part of their interpretation of events post war. However, on any rational examination of the facts, it is clear that by 1918 a series of crippling defeats in the west signalled that it was only a matter of time before the Field Army was destined to suffer a calamitous collapse and a crushing defeat.

German officers posing early in the war. This picture shows them in a carefree time as they play instruments and smile at the camera. Times like these would soon become rare.

July 1913 – Soldiers from the 3. Unter-Elsässisches Infanterie-Regiment Nr. 138 marching at a training area near Oberhofen, prior to the outbreak of war.

The German army had a reserve of a staggering 4.3 million men trained in combat. This was due to the fact that young men spent the years between the ages of 17 to 20 in the Landsturm before they progressed in to the active army or Ersatz reserve, and the fact that all men between 17 and 45 were eligible for military service.

August 1914 – Prussian Guard infantry are given flowers as they head toward the front lines. War is now upon Europe.

The German infantry were a mixture of regular formations and reserve formations. These men are from Landwehr Infantry Regiment Nr. 1.

A wife helps carry her husband's pack as he marches to the train station alongside other German soldiers and their loved ones.

August 1914 – A detachment of the 34th Infantry Brigade from Mecklenburg-Strelitz. Soldiers such as these, who made up the Landstürmanner, would suffer terrible losses during the war.

September 1914 – Early German trenches on the edge of a farmer's field are shown here. The trenches are being manned by the 10th Infantry Brigade, III Armee-Korps (Preußen).

A Landsturmmann or Landwehrmmann from an unknown unit carries a Gew 88 rifle fitted with a Sg 71 bayonet alongside the usual accoutrements such as his rolled blanket and mittens.

September 1914 – Reinforcements from the replacement battalion of Landwehr Infanterie Regiment Nr. 47. Early in the war, Landwehr and Landsturm soldiers often used old uniforms and equipment.

November 1914 – Men of Landsturm Bataillon 'Minden', in Belgium, wearing black or blue fatigues and carrying their trademark Gew 88 rifles fitted with S71 bayonets.

Near the valley of the River Aisne, two soldiers keep guard as their fellows get what sleep they can in the snowy conditions and in their still rather primitive trenches.

Christmas Day 1914, brought an unofficial truce to several stretches of the front. Here we see soldiers from both Britain and Germany fraternizing near Ploegsteert, Belgium, on Christmas Day, an event that was not to be repeated in subsequent years, with only a couple of very small exceptions.

December 1914 – German soldiers make the best of what they have and gather to celebrate Christmas in the field.

Further away from the front, New Year's Eve celebrations look much different, as soldiers enjoy a lighthearted evening.

January 1915 – Artillery munitions column drivers from the 5th Armee Korps are shown here. Their task of supplying shells to the enormous appetite of the guns was essential to the war effort.

Early 1915 – In Belgium, the bridge guard of 56th Infantry Brigade pose in front of their charge, a recently repaired railway bridge.

Early 1915 – Though elaborate looking, the thick winter coats were essential to this Landsturmmann on sentry duty; without suitable attire the freezing night time temperatures could be deadly. Here we see Musketier Heinrich Dalbender shortly before his posting to a line regiment.

A Bavarian 7.7 cm Feldkanone 96 n.A. is shown here in full recoil as its crew man their positions The 7.7 cm Feldkanone 96 n.A. was the most commonly used gun by the Germans by a wide margin.

April 1915 – Saxon Landsturm infantrymen from the 47th Infantry Brigade taking pot shots with their Gew 88 rifles. Their spotless uniform suggests that they have not yet seen much – if any – combat.

The sophisticated German trench systems would prove very troublesome for the Allies, as they were superior in both protecting from enemy shell-fire and from adverse weather conditions. The advantage the Germans had was that their trenches were designed to be semi-permanent, as for much of the war they were on the defensive on the Western Front.

1915 – Heavily armed Bavarian soldiers carrying grenades, rifles and even fighting knives pose for the camera.

1915 – A narrow yet sturdily reinforced trench is crowded with Bavarian infantrymen.

1915 – A newly constructed trench is now home to an infantryman from Landwehr-Infanterie-Regiment Nr. 123

1915 – Six young infantrymen are shown here in this photo taken by Private Fritz Limbach. As you can see, the soldiers have customised their uniform with a non-regulation neckerchief.

June 1915 – Hidden under camouflage netting is a 10 cm Kanone 04/12 with its gun crew (Geschützbedienung) posing for the camera.

1915 – Here we see a German infantryman wielding a Fein electric drill as his companions gaze curiously in to the photographer's lens.

June 1915 – An infanterist from the Kgl. Bayer. 15. Infanterie-Regiment König Friedrich August von Sachsen. Old equipment was still being used in places amongst the German troops, with this soldier's tunic being from 1910. He is carrying a Gew 98 rifle fitted with a rare Bayerisches Seitengewehr M1869/98 bayonet.

A German soldier communicates via field telephone whilst others hold a spool of wire, which will be rolled out as they advance, to allow contact to be maintained as they head in to the field.

This war horse sports a captured Russian Maxim M1910 machine gun, complete with its accompanying wheeled mount and ammunition box. Horse and mule power played a vital part in the war efforts of all the combatant nations.

Clutching their grenades, soldiers from the Landwehr-Infanterie-Regiment Nr. 78, suitably posed, wait anxiously in their trench, ready to repel an attack by Russian forces.

This young Saxon soldier is photographed in his garrison during the time before his deployment to the front. Like so many others in all armies, he would be poorly prepared for the horrors that would await him at the front.

Having received his Iron Cross Second Class from the Kaiser, a proud soldier marches back to his position, carrying the envelope containing his medal.

May 1915 – Infantrymen from Kgl. Sächs. Reserve-Infanterie-Regiment Nr. 102 in their garrison town of Zittau. Four of these five young Saxons carry the Gew 98 rifle.

The crew of a Bavarian 7.7 cm Feldkanone 96. The FK96 was a staple of the Feldartillerie regiments and these guns played a vital role in nearly every battle fought by the Germans during the Great War.

The breech of an antiquated Krupp 15 cm Ringkanone is photographed here, surrounded by its Landsturm Fußartillerie crew.

Sporting a rudimentary gasmask and goggles, this Saxon Unteroffizier is pictured ascending a ladder to a treetop observation platform. This bird's eye view would be valuable in surveillance and warning troops of danger, such as gas attacks.

1915 – In south west Belgium, German soldiers conceal themselves around large haystacks as their commanders make their observations. Given the generally rather relaxed atmosphere and the lack of any shell damage, this was doubtless a training exercise.

1915 – Soldiers from Landwehr Infantry Regiment Nr. 15 are pictured here; some of these men carry the S71 m.S bayonet.

This photograph illustrates the sophistication of German defensive systems. A reinforced concrete structure has been built over the cellar of an existing building to provide shell-proof accommodation. It was a general policy of the Germans to make such shelters in existing buildings as far as possible. Given the defensive nature for much of the war for the German army, it made sense to deploy considerable resources on such shelters; the allies did far less of this type of work.

1915 – Soldiers from the 1. Landsturm Infanterie Bataillon 'Mannheim' sporting Russian M.91 Mosin-Nagants that they have no doubt been captured from fallen enemies. The guns are complete with their socket bayonets (designation EB 147).

Pictured here are a pair of Landsturm infantrymen, they carry an improved version of the Gewehr Prufungs Kommission designed Gew 88 rifle, the Gew 88/05. Given the state of their uniforms, they have yet to see action or are enjoying a prolonged stint away from the front.

Gas attacks struck fear in to the hearts of all soldiers on the battlefields during the Great War. Here, in an exercise, we see members of a medical unit attempting to revive a soldier who has succumbed to a gas attack with a bottle of oxygen. Given the relaxed atmosphere portrayed in the photograph, this is probably an exercise.

December 1915 – This young infantryman in the snow from an unidentified Prussian regiment is equipped with a Gew 98 fitted with a S.98/05 bayonet. Winter conditions were hard on soldiers on both sides of the front.

February 1916 – Taken in the area around Bois de Mort-Mare, this photo displays a group of soldiers from Infanterie-Regiment Nr. 368.

This photograph shows the various stages in the production of the Stahlhelm helmet. The German Army began to replace the traditional boiled leather Pickelhaube with the Stahlhelm during 1916.

A pair of Unteroffiziers from Gebirgs Maschinengewehr Abteilung Nr. 227 sporting the seldom seem 'scroll' helmets. Despite extensive cataloguing of German army uniforms in the Great War, little is known about these helmets and they can be seen in only a few pictures.

27 March 1916 – German prisoners, who have been captured by the Northumberland Fusiliers and Royal Fusiliers, looking surprisingly cheerful at St. Eloi, at the south of the Ypres Salient.

Soldiers from Reserve-Infanterie-Regiment Nr. 212 gather together for a game of cards. A spot of fun in the line, in what appears to be a quiet sector, although danger was never far off.

Shown here are the bombing party or 'Handgranatentrupp' of the 40th Fusilier Regiment. The men carry a variety of equipment, such as S stick-grenades, planks, tools and empty sandbags.

Rats were a persistent problem in the trenches for both German and allied soldiers. German troops here display the corpses of some furry enemies.

April 1916 – Pictured in the ground of their exercise area are Bavarian infantrymen from Kgl. Bayer. 18. Infanterie-Regiment Prinz Ludwig Ferdinand.

30 April 1916 – Bavarian Landsturm Infanterie Bataillon 'Ingolstadt'. These soldiers wear the feldmützen pork-pie caps, marching boots, dark-blue trousers, and simplified Feldrock (tunics), whilst sporting captured Russian M91 rifles and socket bayonets.

Pictured in the centre is a Maschinengewehr 08, or MG 08. These guns were capable of firing 450-500 rounds a minute. The soldier pictured to the rear of the photo holds a model 24 grenade which was often referred to as a 'potato masher'. The one on the right is looking through a trench periscope.

1916 – A Bavarian crew surrounds a 25 cm heavy Minenwerfer (sMW) in northern France. The bomb that it fired contained 47 kilos of TNT, a high-explosive projectile capable of delivering a blast equivalent to the explosive power of 250 7.7 cm artillery shells.

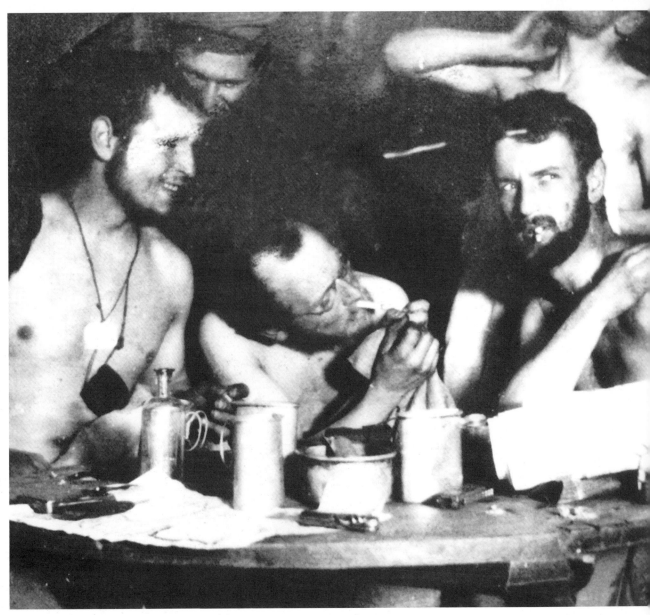

These delousing rituals became commonplace for all soldiers as lice spread rampantly throughout the front. They were a persistent problem for soldiers of all nationalities.

Here German troops attempt to tackle a lice infestation. These were soon ever present among the troops; one way to deal with the problem was to catch them and crush them — they were often found in the seams of clothing — between their fingernails.

An upbeat looking veteran and his companion in a trench shelter, with their equipment hanging at the entrance to the dugout. The man on the right, a 'Frontschwein' – a slang German term for a front line soldier – sports the ribbons of the Iron Cross and another decoration.

In a field exercise, the Draeger Tubben Model 14, a form of mining breathing kit used to access casualties underground, is put through its paces.

German infantry in a shelter wait anxiously for the British bombardment to end during the early stages of the Somme Offensive. The strength and depth of the German dugouts generally proved to be the equal of the British bombardment.

1916 – Soldiers of the Landwehr armed with a variety of weapons including grenades, rifles, bayonets and vicious-looking trench clubs.

1916 – A posed machine gun crew from Kgl. Bayer. 21. Infanterie-Regiment Großherzog Friedrich Franz IV v Mecklenburg-Schwerin with their MG 08 near Vigneulles-lès-Hattonchâtel.

1 July 1916 – In this still taken from the film 'The Battle of the Somme', a guard of the 1st Royal Welch Fusiliers, 22 Brigade, 7th Division is watching captured German prisoners of war at Minden Post.

July 1916 – At Contalmaison, German prisoners are tasked with pushing a water cart out of the mud.

A shell hole between Montauban and Carnoy is filled with the bodies of dead German soldiers.

An entrance to a captured German dugout on the Somme. Many of these had been deepened in the months preceding the battle. The entrance is rather primitive and would unlikely survive a direct hit, hence such dugouts usually had more than one entrance.

An observation balloon rises in to the air behind a motorcycle dispatch rider as he examines the grave of a fallen comrade.

A cradle mounted Gew 98 / M.14 rifle grenade combination is pictured surrounded by soldiers from the Kgl. Sächs. 17. Infanterie-Regiment Nr. 183.

A German soldier throws a hand grenade against enemy positions. Note the mass of barbed wire protecting the trench.

July 1916 – Lewis guns captured by the Germans are carried away in triumph.

A young German soldier engaged in the Battle of the Somme. By July 1916 the only steel helmets available to the German army had been issued to troops on the Verdun front. They began to become available on the Somme in August 1916, but were in short supply. As a result, initially they were handed over between units as trench stores on handover/takeover. For much of the early weeks of the battle, the most common German headgear was the field cap.

Prisoners and guards wait in the trenches as others pass by overhead.

Three portraits of a German prisoners taken by an official British photographer.

Pictured here is a largely youthful group of Bavarian infantrymen sporting the M1916 steel helmet.

Soldiers from the 2MGK L.J.R. 74 (2nd Machine Gun Company Landwehr Infantry Regiment 74) are shown here in a trench in front of a stash of gasmask filters and hand-grenades, essential equipment for the front line soldier.

1916 – A Bavarian Landsturmmann from Landsturm Infanterie Bataillon 'München' (I.B.20) poses here armed with his Gew 98 rifle and wearing the uniform of a line regiment. This soldier's main duties would be in civilian/military worker battalions and guarding the rear echelons.

1916 – Machine gunners from 2. Nassauisches Infanterie-Regiment Nr. 88 undergoing training.

A young soldier from Kgl. Sächs. Reserve-Infanterie-Regiment Nr. 107 is pictured here carrying his Gew 98 rifle and accoutrements, including his Ersatz bayonet and a gas mask.

1916 – On the Vistula River on the Russian front, posed German infantrymen aim their machine guns from their trench. German machine guns caused massive casualties on the Russian army.

A crater field defence provides a measure of protection for some Saxons from an unidentified infantry unit as they take shelter. It is a far cry from the sophisticated design of the usual German system.

An MG 08 section poses during training. The group's work would focus on skills such as range finding, entrenching, weapon handling, sustained fire practice and signalling.

1916 – A 3.7 Gruson-Hotchkiss Revolverkanone anti-aircraft gun is manned by members of a Luftschiffer-Bataillon (Nr. 1) that appear to be near a tethered observation balloon. Its task would have seen to provide defence against attacking fighters.

1916 – Taken on the Western Front, this snapshot shows a glimpse of life in a German reinforced dugout.

11 July 1916 – German casualties scattered at the bottom of a trench taken by the allies.

Captured German soldiers, some of whom were lightly wounded in the fighting, are pictured through barbed wire in a prison cage near Morlancourt.

30 July 1916 – A member of Reserve Infantry Regiment 38, 12th Reserve Division, is given a drink at a British aid post probably located west of Guillemont, where the division had been engaged in heavy fighting.

A German soldier lies prone beside the rotting corpse of a fallen French soldier during the Battle of Verdun. Such scenes were common, as the dead were often left decomposing on the battlefield and conditions made their recovery and burial practically impossible.

A winding German convoy extends into the distance. At the head of these are German officers in a car, flanked by soldiers and horses. The photograph gives a good indication of the inadequacy of the road system for the weight of traffic of all types, especially during an offensive.

NCOs the Infanterie-Regiment No. 358 'relaxing' over a game of cards, though one of their number seems unconcerned by the gas threat. This is a reminder of the terrible and ever present threat that the soldiers faced.

Photographed behind the lines on the Somme is a group of German veteran NCOs.

August 1916 – On a rainy day in north-eastern France, proud soldiers pose with their newly received Iron Cross Second Class (Eisernes Kreuz 2. Klasse) medals.

August 1916 – Bavarian assault troops pose for the camera on the Western Front. One soldier in the middle of the photo carries a boom mounted fire-tube.

August 1916 – A well constructed trench near Lake Drisviaty (on the Eastern Front) occupied by three infantrymen from 7. Ostpreußisches Infanterie-Regiment Nr. 44.

September 1916 – The corpses of unfortunate German soldiers litter a trench at Thiepval.

25 September 1916 – Taken near Ginchy, on the Somme, the photograph shows a diminutive German prisoner being casually escorted to the rear.

13 November 1916 – An escort assists a wounded German soldier along the railway line in the Ancre valley. Note the French cameraman to the right, with other German prisoners beyond him.

Late 1916 – Two soldiers pose for the camera in what was considered an amusing picture. This image was a popular commercial postcard, although it is more likely that the mule's 'gas mask' is actually being used as a chaff bag. Horses and mules were issued with specially designed gas masks.

Late 1916 – Pictured in a trench behind a hand grenade store is a German infantry section wearing the M16 steel helmets. Some soldiers (usually sentries) had reinforcing plates strapped to the front to better protect against head wounds.

Late 1916 — In the background of this photograph are trench shields or Grabenschilder that were originally designed to be carried in to battle by assault troops. They were ineffectual and impractical. However, they were soon put to good use as part of trench defences. In the foreground soldiers from the Landwehr Infanterie Regiment 80 pose in a sandbag lined trench.

Late 1916 – At Verdun, soldiers from the 8. Badisches Infanterie-Regiment Nr. 169 pose for the camera in front of a French periscope and a gas alarm, along with the 'club' to sound it.

On the battlefield of Verdun German soldiers are forced to remove their dead by the car load after suffering tremendous losses. During the ten month battle some 300,000 men lost their lives; and another 400,000 became casualties.

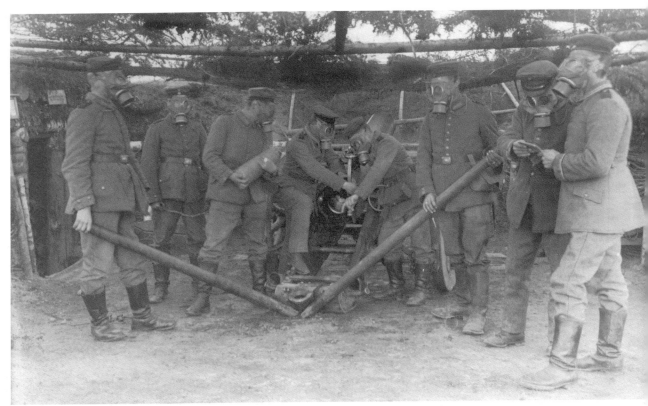

January 1917 – On the Eastern Front, a 15 cm sFH 93 (Schwere Feldhaubitze of 1893) is being loaded by a gun crew from one of the Garde Feldartillerie regiment.

By February 1917 the Verdun front had become relatively quiet. A posed photograph shows members of the German army at full alert.

March 1917 – In the mud in front of a small graveyard are soldiers – possibly from Bavarian Landwehr-Infanterie-Regiment Nr. 7 – standing around a MG 08 heavy machine gun.

Rather unenthusiastic looking Bavarian gunners prepare to set to work in a fairly well protected (by the steep bank) munitions dump some distance from the front.

1917 – Redecorated in German livery, British tanks are put through their paces. It was hoped that tanks with their armour and climbing capability would break the stalemate on the Western Front.

1917 – Two German soldiers support a wounded British prisoner of war. The right leg of the latter's trousers has been ripped open and his puttees have been removed.

1917 – A German soldier dives for cover as a shell explodes behind him in an artillery position.

Taken on the Western Front we see a Flammenwerfer (flame thrower) in action. These fearsome weapons were not particularly effective except as a terror weapon.

April 1917 – During the Battle of the Aisne, a French surprise attack is being brought under enfilade fire by German machine guns.

Prisoners of war – Three youthful looking Germans pose for the camera following their capture. The wounds of two of them have been tended to, but they remain caked in mud, and stare miserably in to the lens.

1917 – A German military kitchen behind the line. Note the presence of women workers, one of whom at least is a nurse. The Germans had a sophisticated system of kitchens and bakeries, as close as practicable to the front line.

In a forward position a Saxon soldier from an unidentified Reserve Infanterie Regiment manages to find a shady seat from which to escape the heat.

May 1917 – A 7.7 cm Flak position near Fontaine-Notre-Dame. The mount is a commonly found ('ortsfest' – static) type and the shells are 7.7 cm M.96 n.A.

June 1917 – Men from an unidentified regiment pose for the camera with their gas masks out of their canisters. This precaution would suggest they are not far from the front.

June 1917 – Members of the Ostfriesisches Feld-Artillerie-Regiment Nr. 62 pose for the camera. A large number of German soldiers favoured British (or British style) puttees to the usual calf length boots, as illustrated by the wounded soldier sitting in the front row.

July 1917 – The chaos and debris on the battlefield could often be utilised to a tactical advantage. Here the crew of a 7.58 cm Leichter Minenwerfer is using a destroyed bunker as a concealed firing platform for their weapon. The soldier on the left has what looks like a spanner around his neck, a tool used to adjust the fuzes on the projectiles.

A large German bunker with an elegantly written name, the Saxon fort. Amongst the debris there are signs of signals wire, whilst the top has a crown of barbed wire.

September 1917 – A tandem bicycle is used as a power generator for a light radio station on the Western Front by a German communications squad.

September 1917 – Gas clouds roll across a training ground as German soldiers practise operating with gas. Chemical weapons were designed to terrorize and incapacitate; however, they became more lethal as new types were introduced as the war progressed.

In this emotional image taken near Havrincourt a German soldier closes the eyes of a fallen comrade whilst others look on.

12 October 1917 – The First Battle of Passchendaele resulted in very heavy losses; the New Zealand Division suffered particularly heavily, enduring over 2,500 casualties of whom over 800 were killed. The sheer destructive power of artillery by this stage of the war is illustrated by the mass of German casualties in the ruins of one of their numerous fortified positions.

October 1917 – Outside a battered bunker near Langemark, captured German officers are guarded by a Scottish soldier.

November 1917 — German soldiers escort captured Italian soldiers to the rear near the town of Kobarid during the Battle of Caporetto.

Winter 1917 – A group of machine gunners from 1. Landsturm Infanterie Bataillon 'Rastatt' (XIV. 5), are pictured with a MG 08 in the snow in the Vosges.

December 1917 – In this photograph taken near the Hochberg (Alsace) is an Offizier-Stellvertreter (Officer-Deputy) from Fußartillerie-Bataillon Nr. 48 surrounded by his NCOs.

27 January 1918 – German officers clowning around during the Kaiser's birthday celebrations in Rauscedo, Italy.

Spring 1918 – German officers pose next to an armoured car in Ukraine.

March 1918 – A horse transport supply column moves through the village of Templeux, crossing paths with advancing German infantry. This illustrates the very considerable pressure that the mass movement of troops and their equipment put on the inadequate road system.

May 1918 – Dead British and German soldiers line this abandoned trench, originally dug by the French. Two German soldiers pick through it, looking for useful items of equipment. The one closest to the camera has commandeered the overcoat of a British sergeant.

1918 – Near St. Quentin on the Western Front, a German messenger dog streaks out of shot, having been loosed by his handler as a gas attack gets underway. Dogs were used by all the sides in the war for a variety of tasks; of all the combatants, the British probably used them least.

1918 – Despatch dogs, probably with their handlers, have their wounds dressed at a dog veterinary centre.

1918 – German troops trying to rescue a French soldier from a mud filled crater, northern France.

April 1918 – Near Villers-Bretonneux, German stromtroopers advance in what would be amongst the last significant effort to achieve victory made by the Germans on the Western Front. Note the dead French soldier on the right of the photo.

June 1918 – Later in the war, gas attacks were an ever present threat. Horses required protection, just as the soldiers did. This horse and his rider are part of a German ammunition column that is preparing to move through a contaminated area.

Parcels from home seem to do little to raise the spirits of the machine gunners from 1. Landsturm Infanterie Bataillon 'Rastatt' (XIV. 5), who are standing in a reserve ammunition store.

1918 – German troops cross a field scarred with shallow trenches en masse.

In a village near Rheims, German A7V tanks move forward, throwing up a mighty cloud of dust.

A rare German A7V tank is loaded on to a railroad flat car on the Western Front. Very few of these tanks were ever produced, less than fifty. German troops found more success using captured allied tanks.

June 1918 – This balloon and its associated equipment, a motor winch and a truck, were captured during the Battle of Soissons.

19 July 1918 – This German soldier washes his clothes next to an array of unfuzed 50 cm shells, in the area between Laon and Soissons.

1918 – The 38 cm SK L/45 or 'Langer Max' was a rapid firing railroad gun that could fire a 750 kg (1,650 lb) high explosive projectile up to 34,200 m (37,400 yd). The soldiers in the foreground are preparing shells for firing, including the filling of a ballistic 'sleeve'.

Rows of gas projectors being loaded by German troops. These would be laid in batches and fired electronically. The range was short; the idea was to create a dense gas (or smoke cloud) as accurately as possible.

A German infantryman, equipped with a newly issued (1916) steel helmet, aims a MG 08 (mounted on a small tripod) from the security of his trench. The sign at the left foreground indicates the boundary between two platoons.

Men of Infanterie-Regiment Vogel von Falkenstein Nr. 56 are photographed on the Western Front aiming their weapons whilst wearing gas masks. They wear the stirnpanzer on the front of their helmets, which helped to protect the front of the head against sniping and other dangers.

Lightly equipped German soldiers moving forward over relatively unscathed country, assisted by a smoke screen.

Near Ripent (Champagne), German storm troops race across the ground to occupy a freshly fired mine crater (above). On occupying (ideally) the furthest lip, work began immediately to secure the position and to develop its defences (below).

Mid 1918 – German soldiers pose around a trio of Mauser 13mm anti-tank rifles often called the 'Tankgewehr M1918' or simply the 'T-Gewehr'. It was the first anti-tank rifle to go into service.

In August 1918 the allies launched what became a series of offensives known as the Hundred Days. Their efforts were rewarded by increasing numbers of German prisoners, as illustrated below.

19 September 1918 — This German machine gunner, photographed near Hargicourt, forward of the main Hindenburg Line defences, fell at his post. Note the belted ammunition and the cases from expended rounds and other equipment for a machine gun, which has already been removed.

German guards use captured British troops to search for and retrieve the personal effects of their comrades killed in battle. In an ideal world, these would eventually find their way back to their families.

A large group of German prisoners being marched along a road somewhere in France by their British guard, as other soldiers look on.

1918 – A lone wagon stands on a damaged road: the horses that pulled it slaughtered and a dead gunner, possibly its driver, slumped across the seat.

1 November 1918 – In Solesmes, north of Le Cateau, German prisoners of war move through the town under the watchful eye of French locals.

4 November 1918 – A young German machine gunner, killed in his position near Villers-devant-Dun, in the American sector. He came within a week of being saved by the Armistice, signed on 11 November.

On the parade ground of a military hospital, German amputees exercise as part of their rehabilitation from war injuries. Thousands of men – millions even – suffered the consequences of their injuries, physical and mental, in the decades after the war ended.